STARTUP BUSINES

Navigating Your First Years As An Entrepreneur

Jerremy Specter-Mendam

Embarking on the entrepreneurial journey is akin to setting sail into uncharted waters, where the allure of discovery is matched only by the tests of resilience. "Startup Business Success" emerges as a beacon for those intrepid souls drawn to the world of entrepreneurship, offering not just a map to navigate these waters but a compass to guide them towards their dreams. Authored by a seasoned navigator of the business world, this book distils years of experience, successes, and lessons into a guide that speaks directly to the heart and mind of the modern entrepreneur.

This is more than a book; it is a mentorship in written form, meticulously crafted to address the multifaceted aspects of building a business from the ground up. The author delves into the essence of what it means to create, innovate, and persevere, blending practical wisdom with strategic insights. "Startup Business Success" breaks down the barriers to entrepreneurship, making the complex journey of business creation accessible, understandable, and, most importantly, achievable.

In today's rapidly evolving economic landscape, agility and foresight are paramount. This book recognizes and addresses

tomorrow. Through a combination of timeless principles and contemporary strategies, "Startup Business Success" equips aspiring entrepreneurs with the tools needed to succeed in a competitive and ever-changing market.

Whether you are at the cusp of launching your first venture or seeking to inject new life into an existing business, this book offers valuable insights that span the spectrum of entrepreneurship. It is a testament to the belief that anyone, with the right guidance and mindset, can navigate the complexities of the business world and emerge victorious.

As you engage with the pages of "Startup Business Success," you embark on a transformative journey of growth and discovery. This book is an invitation to explore the realms of possibility, to challenge the status quo, and to boldly pursue your entrepreneurial vision.

begins here, guided by the wisdom and insights contained within this essential tome.

Welcome aboard the voyage of a lifetime. Welcome to "Startup Business Success."

[Foreword by Jerremy Specter-Mendam, the anonymous CEO]

Validation is the litmus test for your business idea, determining if there's a genuine market need and potential for success.

Market Research: Dive deep into understanding who your competitors are and what they offer. Use online surveys, social media polls, and interviews to gather insights directly from your target audience. Analysing competitors through a SWOT (Strengths, Weaknesses, Opportunities, Threats) analysis can highlight gaps in the market you can exploit.

1.   Identify Your Target Audience:

-       **Example**: A startup creating eco-friendly packaging materials conducts surveys and focus groups within the food and beverage industry. They analyze consumer behavior and preferences on sustainability to define their primary market segment as small to medium-sized organic food producers seeking environmentally friendly packaging solutions.

- **Example**: An emerging mobile app for language learning uses competitive analysis tools to examine the features, pricing models, and user engagement strategies of leading apps in the market. By identifying gaps in language offerings and user experience, they tailor their app to cater to underserved languages and

incorporate gamification for enhanced user engagement.

3.   Assess Market Trends and Demand:

- **Example**: A company planning to launch a new line of smart home devices reviews industry reports, attends technology expos, and monitors social media buzz to gauge consumer interest in smart home

technology. They discover a growing trend towards interoperability among devices and decide to focus on developing products that are compatible with multiple platforms and ecosystems, positioning themselves as a versatile solution in the smart home market.

6

and demonstrate how your solution is different or better. This difference could be in terms of cost, efficiency, ease of use, or accessibility.

1.   Define and Understand the Problem:

-       **Example**: A SaaS company notices a significant drop in user engagement after a recent update. They gather feedback through user surveys and data analytics to pinpoint the issue: a new feature's complexity confuses users. By clearly defining the problem, they focus on simplifying the user interface for that feature.

2.   Generate and Evaluate Potential Solutions:

-       **Example**: An online retailer struggles with high cart abandonment rates. They brainstorm several solutions: introducing a progress indicator, simplifying the checkout process, offering a guest checkout option, and sending abandoned cart emails with a discount offer. Each solution is evaluated based on feasibility, cost, and potential impact on the checkout experience.

- **Example**: After experiencing low attendance at its virtual events, a non-profit organization decides to implement a more interactive platform that allows for real-time engagement and breakout sessions. They promote the new platform's features to their audience and monitor attendance rates and participant feedback after each event. The increased attendance and positive feedback confirm the effectiveness of the chosen solution, demonstrating the importance of adaptability and audience engagement in problem-solving.

Feasibility and Viability: Consider the practical aspects of bringing your product or service to market. This includes looking into manufacturing capabilities, supply chain logistics, and the cost of production. Conduct a break-even analysis to understand when your business might start turning a profit. Assessing feasibility also means considering the legal and regulatory landscape relevant to your business.

Problem:

A startup aims to launch an innovative, solar-powered smartphone that can charge itself using natural light. While the idea is environmentally friendly and addresses the substantial market demand for such a product.

Solution:

Feasibility Analysis:

-       The team conducts a technical feasibility study, consulting with solar technology experts and engineers to assess whether the solar charging feature can be integrated into a smartphone without significantly increasing its size or cost. They explore the latest advancements in solar cell efficiency and lightweight materials.

Market Viability Analysis:

-       To gauge market interest, the startup launches a market research campaign, including online surveys targeted at tech enthusiasts and environmentally conscious consumers. They also analyze market trends towards sustainable products and technologies in the consumer electronics industry.

-       The feasibility analysis reveals that, with current technology, the solar charging feature would make the smartphone prohibitively expensive for the mass market and add considerable bulk to the device's design. However, the market viability analysis indicates strong interest in eco-friendly technology among consumers, suggesting potential for niche markets.

Adapted Solution:

-       Given the technical and cost barriers, the startup decides to pivot. Instead of a fully solar-powered phone, they opt to develop a line of eco-friendly, solar-powered charging accessories compatible with existing smartphones. This approach addresses the identified consumer interest in sustainable technology while remaining technically feasible and financially viable. The startup plans to reinvest profits from the accessories into research for more efficient, cost-effective solar technologies, keeping the vision of a solar-powered phone alive for future development.

A well-crafted business plan is essential for guiding your business's growth and securing funding.

Executive Summary: This section acts as an elevator pitch for your business, offering a snapshot of your mission, vision, the problem you're solving, your solution (product/service), and key financial highlights. It should be compelling enough to entice further reading.

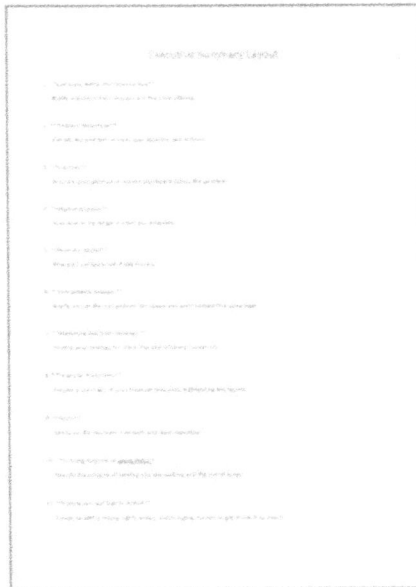

trends and patterns, and explain how your business will set itself apart within this landscape.

DEEP DIVE:

Market analysis is a critical component of business strategy that provides entrepreneurs and businesses with valuable insights into the competitive landscape, customer preferences, and overall market trends. This analysis enables companies to make informed decisions, tailor their products and marketing strategies, and identify opportunities for growth and innovation.

Understanding the Market Landscape

At its core, market analysis involves a deep dive into the dynamics of your target market. This includes understanding the size of the market, growth trends, and the factors driving these trends. For example, a startup in the alternative protein sector might examine the increasing consumer demand for plant-based products, supported by statistics showing a projected global market value of $162 billion for plant-based foods by 2030, according to Bloomberg Intelligence. This data not only validates the market's potential but also highlights the importance of

Competitor Analysis

An essential part of market analysis is assessing the competition. This means identifying who your competitors are, what they offer, and how they position themselves in the market. Take, for instance, the rise of direct-to-consumer (D2C) mattress companies like Casper and Purple. These companies disrupted the traditional mattress retail sector by offering convenient online purchasing options, extended trial periods, and efficient delivery. By analyzing these competitors' strategies, new entrants can identify gaps in the market, such as opportunities for products targeting specific demographics or offering unique features like customizable firmness levels.

Customer Segmentation and Preferences

Market analysis also involves segmenting your target audience and understanding their preferences and behaviors. For a mobile app developer focused on mental wellness, this might involve segmenting the market into groups based on age, lifestyle, and specific mental health needs, like anxiety

most valued by each segment, such as guided meditations for stress relief among working professionals or interactive journals for college students.

Airbnb's rise from a small startup to a global platform for lodging and experiences showcases the power of effective market analysis. Initially, the founders identified a gap in the market for affordable, unique lodging options that provided a more local and personal travel experience than traditional hotels. They validated this market need through early experiments during large conferences in San Francisco when hotel rooms were scarce. The success of these experiments, coupled with data on increasing travel expenditures and a growing interest in authentic travel experiences, guided Airbnb's strategy. The company continuously analyzes market trends, competitor offerings, and customer feedback to innovate and expand its services, such as adding Airbnb Experiences to cater to the demand for local, authentic travel activities.

LESSON LEARNED:

Market analysis is not a one-time task but an ongoing process that requires businesses to stay agile and responsive to changing market dynamics. By thoroughly understanding the market landscape, analyzing competitors, and tuning into customer preferences, businesses can navigate challenges, seize opportunities, and drive sustainable growth. Whether you're an indispensable tool in your strategic arsenal.

Organization and Management: Describe the organizational structure, detailing the roles and experiences of key team members. This section can also include information about the legal structure of your business (e.g., sole proprietorship, partnership, corporation).

Understanding the Structure

At the heart of the Organization and Management section is a clear depiction of the business's organizational structure. This often includes an organizational chart that visually represents relationships between different roles and departments. For instance, a tech startup might display a flat organizational structure, emphasizing agility and open communication channels between the development team and executive officers, encouraging innovation and rapid decision-making.

Detailing Roles and Responsibilities

A comprehensive breakdown of roles and responsibilities is essential. This part goes beyond listing job titles; it dives into the company would not only oversee the technology strategy but also be responsible for aligning the tech stack with business goals, ensuring scalability, and leading the development team towards innovative solutions.

Highlighting Management Team Qualifications

This section shines a light on the management team's qualifications, underscoring the human capital that powers the company. Sharing stories of key team members, their career milestones, previous successful ventures, and specific expertise they bring to the table can significantly bolster investor confidence. Consider a scenario where a biotech startup highlights its CEO's background in leading several successful clinical trials and securing FDA approvals, directly correlating leadership expertise with the company's potential for success.

Operational Strategies

Operational strategies outline how the management plans to achieve business objectives. This might include descriptions of daily operations, supply chain management, quality control measures, and customer service protocols. For a manufacturing quality can illustrate a well-thought-out operational plan poised for efficiency and growth.

"The Organization and Management section of a business plan is not just an administrative overview; it's a strategic component that demonstrates how the company's leadership and operational framework are equipped to execute the business strategy successfully. By detailing the organizational structure, elucidating roles and responsibilities, showcasing the management team's credentials, and outlining operational strategies, this section provides a comprehensive look into the company's operational backbone, setting the stage for sustainable growth and success."

-       **Products or Services**: Go beyond a simple description of your offerings. Explain the benefits to the customer, the product lifecycle, and any research and development activities that may lead to new products or services.

In the "Products or Services" section of a business plan, detailing what your company offers is crucial for understanding your value proposition. Here are some fictional examples to illustrate how diverse this section can be:

1. Eco-Friendly Packaging Solutions - "GreenPack"

Description: GreenPack specializes in biodegradable and compostable packaging solutions designed for the food and beverage industry. Our range includes plant-based containers, cups, and utensils that decompose within 90 days, offering a sustainable alternative to traditional plastic packaging.

Unique Features:

-        Made from renewable resources like cornstarch and bamboo.

\- 	Partnerships with reforestation projects, planting a tree for every 10,000 units sold.

2. Smart Fitness Mirror - "FitView"

Description: FitView is an interactive smart mirror that brings a personal trainer into your home. Offering live and on-demand fitness classes, real-time feedback on your form, and personalized workout plans, FitView is the future of home fitness.

-        Advanced AI technology that analyzes movements and provides corrective feedback.

-        Integration with health apps to track progress and adjust workout plans.

-        Sleek design that blends into your home décor when not in use.

3. Online Learning Platform for Creative Skills - "CreateSpace"
Description: CreateSpace is an online learning platform offering courses in photography, graphic design, writing, and more, taught by industry professionals. With interactive lessons, peer feedback, and real-world projects, we empower learners to develop their creative skills.

-    A project-based learning approach that focuses on creating a portfolio.

-    Community features for networking, collaboration, and feedback.

-    Partnerships with creative software companies to offer discounted tools for learners.

4. Gourmet Meal Kit Delivery Service - "ChefBox"

Description: ChefBox delivers gourmet meal kits directly to your door, featuring recipes from world-renowned chefs. With pre-measured ingredients, step-by-step instructions, and a focus on international cuisine, ChefBox makes gourmet cooking accessible to everyone.

Unique Features:

-       Options for dietary preferences, including vegan, gluten-free, and keto.

-       Packaging made from 100% recyclable materials to minimize environmental impact.

5. Augmented Reality App for Education - "EduVision"

Description: EduVision is an augmented reality app designed to enhance learning for students of all ages. By bringing subjects like history, science, and art to life through immersive experiences, EduVision makes learning interactive and engaging.

Unique Features:
-       Collaborative projects that encourage learning through exploration and discovery.

-       Customizable learning paths for different educational levels and interests.

-       Partnerships with museums and educational institutions to offer exclusive content.

Services" section can effectively showcase what a company offers, highlighting unique features and the value provided to customers.

Marketing and Sales Strategy: Outline how you plan to attract and retain customers. Discuss your marketing channels (digital marketing, social media, traditional advertising), pricing strategy, sales tactics, and customer service approach.

The marketing and sales strategy is a very key aspect of your business' success!

There's an old quote, **"best known beats best product!"**

This will be the driver for bringing customers to your door! Some people say spend a lot on marketing for awareness, whilst others say be cost-effective and efficient! With that said, having an understanding of your target market will help determine the best method of attack.

Find the strategy that suits your company AS WELL AS your business compass and mission!

Financial Projections: Provide a clear financial forecast that includes sales, costs, and profitability over the next three to five years. Use graphs and charts to make data more accessible. Highlight any assumptions you've made in your projections.

Appendix: This is a place for supporting documents. Include any licenses, patents, resumes of key management, market studies, technical product descriptions, and letters of support from future customers or partners.

Validating and Refining Your Plan

Feedback is invaluable at this stage. Present your business plan to mentors, advisors, or potential customers. Be prepared for constructive criticism and use it to refine your plan. Networking events and entrepreneurial forums can be great places to seek diverse opinions and insights.

This process not only sharpens your focus but also equips you with the knowledge and tools to navigate the complexities of starting and growing a successful enterprise. Each section of your plan should reflect a deep understanding of your market, a clear vision for your business, and a realistic pathway to achieving your goals.

Effective financial Effective financial management is the backbone of any successful startup, ensuring you have the resources needed to grow and sustain your business. management is the backbone of any successful startup, ensuring you have the resources needed to grow and sustain your business.

Understanding Startup Costs

Knowing the initial costs is crucial for setting a realistic budget and securing funding.

Fixed vs. Variable Costs: Distinguish between fixed costs (rent, salaries) and variable costs (materials, shipping). This understanding helps in budgeting and forecasting.

Capital Expenditures: Include one-time costs for assets like equipment or property. These investments often have a significant impact on your initial budget.

cash flow in the early stages.

Reserve Fund: Recommend setting aside a reserve fund to cover unexpected expenses or downturns in revenue. This financial cushion can be vital for navigating the first year.

Securing Funding

Explore various funding options to identify the best fit for your startup's needs and stage of development.

Bootstrapping: Starting with personal savings or income from early sales. This option keeps you in control but may limit growth speed.

Angel Investors: Wealthy individuals willing to invest in promising startups in exchange for equity. Networking and pitch events are common ways to meet angel investors.

Venture Capital: For startups with high growth potential, venture capitalists provide significant funding and resources but often require a substantial equity stake.

early access to products or exclusive rewards.

Loans: Traditional bank loans or SBA loans can be options, though they require a strong business plan and often personal collateral.

Budgeting and Financial Planning

Creating a detailed budget helps manage your finances effectively, ensuring sustainability and growth.

Revenue Projections: Estimate your sales for the first year, considering market research and industry benchmarks. Be conservative to avoid overestimating.

Cash Flow Management: Monitor cash flow closely. Use tools or software to track income and expenses, ensuring you always have enough cash on hand to cover obligations.

Break-Even Analysis: Calculate the point at which your business becomes profitable. This is crucial for understanding when you might expect to start seeing a return on your investment.

Identify and monitor key financial metrics to gauge your business's health and guide decision-making.

Gross Margin: Measures the profitability of your products or services after the cost of goods sold is deducted.

Customer Acquisition Cost (CAC): The cost associated with acquiring a new customer. Keeping this lower than the lifetime value of a customer ensures profitability.

Burn Rate: The rate at which your company consumes cash. Particularly important for startups that are pre-revenue or expanding rapidly.

budgeting, and keeping a close eye on financial metrics. These practices are not just about keeping your startup afloat but about setting the stage for sustainable growth and success. With a clear financial plan and the discipline to stick to it, you'll be well-equipped to make informed decisions that propel your business forward."

"Building a brand and establishing an online presence is an ongoing process that requires consistency, creativity, and attention to detail. By carefully crafting your brand identity, launching a user-friendly website, engaging actively on social media, and utilizing email marketing, you set the foundation for lasting relationships with your customers and a strong position in the digital marketplace. This chapter equips you with the strategies to not just launch your brand but to make it thrive in the competitive online ecosystem."

Creating a compelling brand and robust online presence is pivotal for startups looking to carve out their niche in the digital age.

Define Your Brand Identity: Start by defining your brand values, personality, and unique value proposition. What makes your business stand out? This clarity helps inform all other branding decisions.

Logo and Design Elements: Develop a memorable logo and consistent design elements (color scheme, typography). These should reflect your brand identity and appeal to your target audience.

Brand Voice and Messaging: Establish a consistent brand voice and messaging strategy. Whether it's professional, playful, or inspirational, ensure it resonates with your audience and reflects your brand values.

Your brand is more than your

logo;

it's the essence of your

business!

Your website is often the first point of contact with potential customers, making its design and functionality critical.

User-Friendly Design: Ensure your website is easy to navigate, mobile-friendly, and fast-loading. A positive user experience can significantly affect visitor engagement and conversions.

Content: Populate your site with engaging, valuable content that speaks to your audience's needs and interests. Include clear calls to action (CTAs) to guide users towards making a purchase or contacting you.

SEO: Implement basic search engine optimization (SEO) practices to improve your visibility in search engine results. Use relevant keywords, optimize meta tags, and regularly update your site with fresh content.

Establishing a Social Media Presence

Social media platforms offer powerful channels to build relationships and engage with your audience.

not, social media is a vital tool that can help you grow and succeed! If the majority of the market are using it – then it means you must too to ensure you maximise your attention!

"MONEY

FOLLOWS

ATTENTION"

Choose the Right Platforms: Not all social media platforms are suitable for every business. Select platforms where your target audience is most active and which align with your brand's nature.

messaging across platforms.

Engagement Strategy: Develop a content plan that includes regular posts, interactive elements, and engagement tactics (like responding to comments and messages). Use these platforms to tell your brand's story, showcase your products or services, and connect with your audience on a personal level.

Email Marketing

Email marketing remains one of the most effective ways to reach and engage your audience.

Build Your List: Encourage website visitors to subscribe to your mailing list through sign-up forms, offering incentives like discounts or valuable content.

Segmentation and Personalization: Segment your email list based on subscriber behavior or demographics to tailor messages more effectively. Personalized emails tend to have higher open and conversion rates.

subscribers. Mix promotional messages with informative or entertaining content to keep engagement high.

To build a robust marketing foundation, it's essential to dive deeper into each strategy, understanding not just the basics but also advanced tactics that can set your startup apart.

MARKETING

Delving deeper into each marketing strategy reveals the complexity and potential of effective marketing for new entrepreneurs. By embracing advanced content marketing techniques, leveraging SEO to its fullest, engaging authentically on social media, and maximizing the personalization and efficiency of email marketing, you can build a powerful marketing machine that drives growth and builds lasting relationships with your audience. Remember, the key is not just to execute these strategies but to continuously test, learn, and adapt based on data and feedback.

Content marketing is not just about producing content; it's about creating value and building authority in your niche.

Content Planning and Calendar: Develop a content calendar that aligns with industry events, seasonal trends, and your product launch schedule. Anticipation builds engagement.

User-Generated Content (UGC): Encourage your audience to contribute content related to your brand. UGC can increase engagement and trust, as it comes directly from peers.

Content Repurposing: Transform your existing content into new formats. Turn blog posts into videos, infographics, or podcast episodes to maximize reach and engagement.

Advanced SEO strategies can significantly improve your site's visibility and organic search traffic.

Technical SEO: Ensure your website's technical aspects are optimized for search engines. This includes site speed, mobile-friendliness, and structured data for enhanced snippets in search results.

Local SEO: For businesses serving specific locales, optimize your online presence for local search. Claim your Google My Business listing, encourage local reviews, and include local keywords in your content.

Content Depth and Quality: Google favors content that provides comprehensive answers to search queries. Aim for in-depth articles that cover topics thoroughly, including long-tail keywords and related terms.

To stand out on social media, focus on strategies that foster genuine community and engagement.

Live Video and Stories: Utilize live video and stories to connect with your audience in real-time. These formats offer a raw, unedited look into your brand, building authenticity.

Influencer Collaborations: Partner with influencers who align with your brand values. Their endorsement can introduce your brand to new audiences in a trustworthy context.

Social Listening: Monitor social media for mentions of your brand, industry trends, and relevant conversations. Engaging in these discussions can improve your brand's visibility and authority.

Leveraging personalization and automation can make your email marketing efforts more effective and efficient.

Advanced Segmentation: Use behavioral data (website interactions, purchase history) to segment your list. Tailoring content based on behavior can significantly improve engagement and conversion rates.

Automated Email Series: Set up automated email sequences for different segments or actions (e.g., welcome series, post-purchase follow-up, cart abandonment). These can help nurture leads and increase customer lifetime value.

Securing sales and acquiring customers are critical for the growth and sustainability of your startup. Here, we delve into sophisticated strategies that go beyond basic practices to enhance your sales efforts and customer acquisition processes.

Crafting a Compelling Value Proposition

Your value proposition is the core reason why customers should choose your product or service over competitors. It should be clear, concise, and compelling.

Differentiation: Highlight what makes your offering unique. Is it the quality, price, innovation, or customer service? Make sure this differentiation is evident in all your marketing and sales materials.

Benefits Over Features: Focus on how your product or service benefits the customer rather than just listing its features. Benefits address the customer's problem or need and explain how your offering provides the solution.

their feedback to refine it for maximum impact.

Optimizing the Sales Funnel

A well-optimized sales funnel guides potential customers from awareness to decision-making efficiently.

Awareness: Use targeted marketing campaigns to attract potential customers to your funnel. Content marketing, SEO, and social media are effective channels for building awareness.

Interest and Evaluation: Engage interested prospects with more detailed information about your product or service, such as case studies, demos, or customer testimonials. Email marketing and retargeting ads can be particularly effective here.

Decision and Action: Simplify the decision-making process with clear pricing, compelling offers, and a straightforward purchasing process. Live chat support, FAQs, and comparison guides can help address last-minute doubts.

Building strong relationships with your customers can turn them into advocates for your brand, driving organic growth.

Personalization: Use customer data to personalize interactions and offers. Personalization can increase customer satisfaction and loyalty.

Customer Service Excellence: Provide exceptional customer service that exceeds expectations. Happy customers are more likely to recommend your business to others.

Referral Programs: Implement referral programs that reward customers for bringing in new business. This not only acquires new customers but also reinforces the loyalty of existing ones.

Data-driven strategies allow for more targeted and effective customer acquisition efforts.

Customer Segmentation: Segment your target market based on demographics, behavior, or purchase history. Tailored messages to each segment can improve conversion rates.

Analytics and Metrics: Monitor key metrics such as customer acquisition cost (CAC), lifetime value (LTV), and conversion rates. Use this data to optimize your marketing and sales strategies.

A/B Testing: Continuously test different aspects of your sales and marketing strategies to see what works best. This includes testing marketing messages, sales tactics, and even product features.

Sales and customer acquisition are the lifeblood of any startup. By crafting a compelling value proposition, optimizing your sales funnel, leveraging customer relationships, and utilizing data-driven strategies, you can effectively grow your customer base and scale your business. Remember, the most successful entrepreneurs are those who remain agile, always ready to adapt their strategies based on customer feedback and market trends.

The path of entrepreneurship is rarely smooth, but facing challenges head-on can lead to significant growth and innovation. This chapter explores strategies for overcoming common obstacles and leveraging setbacks as opportunities for learning and development.

Embracing Failure as a Learning Opportunity

Failure is not the opposite of success; it's a part of the journey to success. Understanding and embracing this can transform how you approach challenges.

Analyze Failures: When setbacks occur, take the time to thoroughly analyze what went wrong and why. This reflection can provide valuable insights that prevent future mistakes.

Foster a Growth Mindset: Cultivate a mindset that views failure as an opportunity to grow and learn. Encourage this attitude within your team to build resilience.

support and advice, and help others learn from your journey.

Managing Financial Difficulties

Cash flow issues and financial missteps are common challenges for startups. Effective management strategies can help navigate these troubles.

Regular Financial Reviews: Conduct regular reviews of your finances to identify potential issues early. This includes monitoring cash flow, expenses, and revenue streams.

Flexible Budgeting: Be prepared to adjust your budget based on actual performance and market conditions. A flexible approach can help you allocate resources more effectively.

Seek Expert Advice: Don't hesitate to consult with financial advisors or mentors when facing financial difficulties. Professional advice can be invaluable in formulating a turnaround strategy.

GET AN ACCOUNTANT

Entrepreneurial burnout can affect both you and your team, impacting productivity and morale.

Recognize the Signs: Be aware of burnout symptoms, such as chronic fatigue, irritability, and a decline in performance. Recognizing these early can help address the issue before it escalates.

Implement Work-Life Balance: Encourage a culture that values work-life balance. This can include flexible work hours, regular breaks, and ensuring that workloads are manageable.

Self-Care and Support: Prioritize self-care and seek support when needed. This can involve taking time off, pursuing hobbies, or talking to a mentor or coach.

Overcoming Market and Industry Challenges

Market trends and industry changes can pose significant challenges. Staying adaptable and informed can help you navigate these uncertainties.

adapt your strategies accordingly.

Innovate and Pivot: Be open to pivoting your business model or product offerings in response to market changes. Innovation is key to staying relevant and competitive.

Build Strategic Partnerships: Forming alliances with other businesses can provide mutual support and open up new opportunities, helping to mitigate the impact of market challenges.

Navigating challenges and setbacks is an integral part of the entrepreneurial experience. By learning from failures, managing financial difficulties, addressing burnout, and adapting to market changes, you can build a resilient and flexible business capable of weathering the ups and downs of startup life. Remember, the most successful entrepreneurs are those who view challenges not as roadblocks but as stepping stones to greater achievements.

Success in entrepreneurship goes beyond just strategies, plans, and skills. The underlying attitudes and mindsets of entrepreneurs play a pivotal role in determining their resilience, adaptability, and ultimately, their success.

Cultivating a Positive Attitude

Maintaining a positive attitude helps entrepreneurs see opportunities in challenges and remain motivated in the face of setbacks.

Optimism: Foster an optimistic outlook towards your business and the future. This doesn't mean ignoring reality but choosing to focus on potential solutions rather than dwelling on problems.

Gratitude: Practice gratitude by acknowledging and appreciating the progress you've made and the support you've received. This can enhance your mental wellbeing and strengthen your relationships with your team and network.

can be a powerful motivator during tough times.

Developing a Growth Mindset

A growth mindset, a concept popularized by psychologist Carol Dweck, is the belief that abilities and intelligence can be developed through dedication and hard work.

Embrace Challenges: View challenges as opportunities to grow and learn rather than insurmountable obstacles. This approach encourages innovation and problem-solving.

Learn from Criticism: Constructive criticism is a valuable source of feedback. Approach it with an open mind and a willingness to improve, rather than defensiveness.

Celebrate Effort and Progress: Recognize and celebrate the effort and progress, not just outcomes. This reinforces the value of perseverance and hard work.

Resilience: Bouncing Back Stronger

business with determination.

Build a Support Network: Cultivate a network of mentors, peers, and advisors who can offer guidance, support, and perspective when challenges arise.

Maintain Physical and Mental Health: Regular exercise, a healthy diet, and mindfulness practices can improve your resilience by enhancing your overall wellbeing.

Adaptability: Stay flexible and open to change. The ability to pivot and adapt strategies in response to feedback and market changes is crucial for long-term success.

"The journey of entrepreneurship is as much about internal growth as it is about building a business. Cultivating a positive attitude, a growth mindset, and resilience can empower you to face challenges with courage, learn from your experiences, and pursue your vision with unwavering passion. These qualities not only enhance your potential for success but also contribute to a fulfilling and impactful entrepreneurial journey. Embrace the power of attitude and mindset, and let them be the guiding forces on your path to success."

- How to use this workbook

Read through each chapter and apply your business strategy with the following in mind! Now you have absorbed the information – start putting it into practice! We suggest getting a blank notepad and pen and mapping out each section on a new page.

- Goal setting exercise

Your goal is to complete a workbook section for each chapter in a specified timeframe! Give yourself one day, one week, or one month per chapter to detail this workbook! Whatever it is – be sure to use the SMART Goals in mind:

Specific

Measurable

Accountable

Realistic

Timely

- Activity 1: Idea Validation Checklist

- Exercise: Budgeting Basics - Create Your First Startup Budget

.

- Activity: Develop Your Brand Identity (Mission, Vision, Values)

- Task: Outline Your Content Marketing Plan

- Exercise: Growth Mindset vs. Fixed Mindset – Identifying Your Beliefs

1.   **Define the Problem Your Idea Solves**: List out the key problems and how your product/service offers a solution.

2.   **Identify Your Target Market**: Who are they? What do they need?

3.   **Conduct Market Research**: Outline steps to gather data on your idea's potential.

4.   **Feedback Mechanism**: How will you collect feedback on your idea? Plan a small focus group or survey.

Sample Exercise: Budgeting Basics

1.   **List Your Estimated Startup Costs**: Include everything from legal fees, branding, to initial inventory.

2.   **Monthly Operating Expenses**: Estimate your recurring costs.

4.   **Break-even Analysis**: Using the above numbers, calculate how long until your startup potentially breaks even.

This workbook is designed to be an interactive companion to your book, helping readers apply what they've learned directly to their entrepreneurial endeavors. Each activity encourages practical thinking and real-world application, ensuring that by the end of the workbook, the reader has a solid foundation for starting their business journey.

These case studies are for your benefit and to be used as examples and inspiration only. Learn from these and become your own case study!

Case Study 1: EcoTech Innovations - Embracing Sustainability

Challenge: EcoTech Innovations, a startup focused on renewable energy solutions, struggled to differentiate itself in a crowded market and secure initial funding.

Strategy: The company decided to leverage its commitment to sustainability not just as a product feature but as a core brand identity. They invested in community-based renewable projects and partnered with environmental organizations.

Outcome: EcoTech Innovations gained significant media attention for its projects, leading to increased investor interest. Their community-focused approach also attracted a loyal customer base, driving initial sales and establishing the company as a leader in sustainable energy solutions.

Challenge: QuickMeal entered the competitive food delivery space but found it challenging to compete with established players on speed and price.

Strategy: Instead of competing directly on common metrics, QuickMeal focused on niche markets, specifically health-conscious consumers and dietary-specific meals. They also implemented AI-driven logistics optimization.

Outcome: By carving out a unique market position and enhancing operational efficiency, QuickMeal saw a 40% increase in order volume within six months, significantly improving profit margins and customer satisfaction.

Challenge: SafeGuard AI developed an innovative personal security device but struggled with consumer adoption due to high product costs and market skepticism.

Strategy: The startup launched an educational campaign highlighting the technology's benefits and real-world applications. They offered a subscription model to lower upfront costs.

Outcome: The educational campaign raised awareness and trust in the product, while the subscription model made it more accessible. Sales increased by 60%, and subsequent funding rounds were highly successful.

Challenge: LearnAnywhere, an online learning platform, faced difficulties standing out in the rapidly growing e-learning sector.

Strategy: They focused on offering highly customizable learning paths and incorporating adaptive learning technologies to personalize the education experience.

Outcome: The unique selling proposition of personalized learning attracted both learners and educators, resulting in a tripled user base and partnerships with several educational institutions.

Challenge: GreenBuild created a revolutionary green construction material but found market entry challenging due to the construction industry's reluctance to adopt new materials.

Strategy: GreenBuild targeted small-scale projects and partnered with eco-friendly builders for pilot projects, showcasing the material's benefits and sustainability impact.

Outcome: Success in initial projects led to increased interest from larger construction firms. GreenBuild secured several high-profile contracts, and the company is now a recognized innovator in sustainable construction materials.

Each case study provides a snapshot of how startups can navigate challenges through strategic thinking, innovation, and a focus on their core strengths, offering valuable lessons for new entrepreneurs.

Future Trends and Predictions: Navigating Tomorrow's Business Landscape

As we stand on the brink of a new era in business innovation and strategy, it's imperative for entrepreneurs and business leaders to look ahead, anticipating the waves of change that will reshape the competitive landscape. This section delves into emerging trends and predictions that are poised to influence the future of startups and established businesses alike. Understanding these dynamics will equip you to adapt, innovate, and thrive in the evolving market.

The Rise of AI and Automation

Artificial Intelligence (AI) and automation are not just buzzwords; they are revolutionizing how businesses operate, offering unprecedented efficiencies, insights, and capabilities. From automating routine tasks to providing deep analytical insights and enabling personalized customer experiences, AI is set to become an integral part of business strategy. Predictions suggest that companies embracing AI will not only streamline operations but also unlock new avenues for innovation and customer engagement.

As global awareness of environmental issues grows, consumers are increasingly prioritizing sustainability and ethical considerations in their purchasing decisions. Businesses that adopt sustainable practices, from reducing carbon footprints to ensuring fair trade and labor practices, will gain a competitive edge. The trend towards sustainability is also driving innovation in product development, supply chain management, and corporate social responsibility.

Remote Work and Digital Nomadism

The pandemic has accelerated the shift towards remote work, a trend that's expected to persist. This shift has implications for everything from office space requirements to team management, collaboration technologies, and corporate culture. Businesses will need to adapt to this new normal by creating flexible work policies, investing in digital collaboration tools, and rethinking their approach to team engagement and productivity.

As businesses become increasingly digital, the threat landscape evolves with them. Cybersecurity will move from being a specialized concern to a central element of business strategy. Protecting customer data, ensuring the integrity of operations, and complying with regulatory requirements will require robust cybersecurity measures. Businesses that prioritize and effectively manage cybersecurity risks will build stronger trust with customers and partners.

Decentralization and Blockchain

Blockchain technology is paving the way for decentralized business models that offer transparency, security, and efficiency. Beyond cryptocurrency, blockchain applications in supply chain management, digital identity verification, and secure transactions are emerging. Businesses exploring blockchain solutions can unlock new levels of efficiency, trust, and customer value.

The future of business lies in delivering personalized, seamless customer experiences. Advances in data analytics, machine learning, and interactive technologies will enable businesses to understand and anticipate customer needs like never before. Companies that leverage these insights to deliver tailored products, services, and experiences will stand out in crowded markets.

Lifelong Learning and Skill Development

The rapid pace of technological change necessitates continuous learning and skill development for both entrepreneurs and their teams. Businesses that foster a culture of learning and provide opportunities for professional growth will attract and retain top talent. Furthermore, staying abreast of emerging trends, technologies, and business models will be critical for long-term success.

Navigating the future of business requires a forward-looking mindset,

openness to innovation, and a commitment to adaptability. By understanding and anticipating these trends, you can position your startup or established business for success in the dynamic marketplace of tomorrow. The journey ahead is filled with opportunities for those ready to embrace change and lead the way into the future.

This page is intentionally left blank.

www.ingramcontent.com/pod-product-compliance
Lightning Source LLC
Chambersburg PA
CBHW071439210326
41597CB00020B/3868